THE CRUCIFIXION OF JUDAS

AND OTHER REFLECTIONS ON THE JOURNEY FROM THE MIND TO THE SOUL

BY

TONY BUCK

PLANET PUBLISHING
Pennsylvania, USA

Dedicated to

All those whose faith has been shaken

Acknowledgements

Through the years many have helped me with my writing education, and I'd like to thank them all. Thanks also to those who encouraged me. Thanks to Sally for the dedicated editing. Special thanks, to Bawa Muhaiyaddeen, who taught us the real purpose of human existence, and how to get there.

Contents

Introduction

What is the purpose of religion? I believe it is to get close to God. Not a sky god, but the omniscient, omnipotent, omnipresent, un-created power of the universe. I met a person of wisdom forty-two years ago who knew how to do that. Not only to get close, but also to merge with God, to become what's known as Man-God, God-Man. Man in this case being the zenith of human spiritual attainment, therefore non-gender.

By contemplating that Jesus didn't get crucified, and in fact lived on to teach more, I came up with this storyline. It helped me share my reflections on the thousands of years of the monotheistic tradition. I also share some of my deep imaginings and insights from the last forty-two years. Thirdly, I introduce the "Know Thyself Curriculum," that I think all prophets, saints, and wise people taught to their closest students.

This curriculum, was given to me by my teacher, Bawa Muhaiyaddeen, with whom I lived from 1980 until 1986 when he died. I want people from all spiritual traditions to have access to this, because I don't see how one can merge with God without this depth of self-discovery. I especially wrote this for all those whose faith has been shaken. It is my wish to re-invigorate you, by showing that the divine knowledge of our traditions may have some gaps that we need to fill. I hope you'll agree, when you read this book, that the deep spiritual insights I've shared here are needed on the path to God.

THE CRUCIFIXION
OF JUDAS

1

Am I a Christian?

Am I a Christian? Hesitating, I say, probably not in the way you would recognize. I believe Jesus existed. I follow the spirit of the parables attributed to him, but I don't go along with it all. For instance, and don't think me naïve – I know the world is cruel and that many prophets and wise people were persecuted – but I don't think Jesus was crucified. I think it was Judas who ended up on the cross. I imagine that when the soldiers came to get Jesus on the mount of olive groves, as the story goes, he'd gone further up the mount, leaving the disciples sleeping. So these military kidnappers start looking around while waking everyone. Don't forget it is pitch dark, except for the light from the flaming torches they're carrying. Have you ever been in total darkness? So many people haven't today. Perhaps on a camping trip or in a cave?

Now Judas is supposed to identify Jesus, and he's busy looking around but can't find him. He begins to panic, and the arresting soldiers say, "Well we can't go back empty handed." They probably weren't present when the plot was being hatched, so they don't know who Judas or any of them are. I've been in religious communities with gurus and such, and there are always a few who want to be the guru. So they dress and cut their hair and beard like him, and sometimes even fool people. Now I think Judas was one of those, full of envy. He wanted to be the holy one but not prepared or even capable of doing the 'inner work' necessary to obtain the exalted state. So I could see one of the soldiers finger Judas saying, "He's the one, I've seen him before."

Judas of course would protest, and the more he denies it, the more convinced they become he is the one they seek. The other disciples stay out of it, not knowing what is going on or wishing to be implicated in the presence of these agents of fascism of an unforgiving system. Now, the soldiers convince themselves they can't go back empty handed, as they will get it in the neck. So they take Judas, and that's how I think it all begins.

"Wait," you say. "Then what happens to Jesus?" Well, in fear and confusion, I think all the disciples and whoever else was there, disperse immediately, not wanting to be associated with what's happened. A little later, Jesus returns to that spot and finds no one there. Now, of course, I consider Jesus divinely wise and merged with God. I had the privilege and experience of knowing someone of that caliber years ago, so I know he has the inner intuition as to what might have happened. After all, he would know all his disciples intimately, and he would know the scheming that was in Judas' heart.

Realizing that this time had finally arrived, I think he would seek out Mary, his mother, who might be staying in a relative's house nearby. Obviously Mary would be very relieved to see him. She tells him there are already rumors that soldiers have arrested him and possibly other companions, including Judas. Well, you can imagine they would fall into discussing the situation, perhaps realizing that Jesus' mission in Jerusalem was over. No longer safe for him or his associates. So the question would be, what's the next chapter of their lives?

2

Why these ideas?

I'm seventy-two now, and I've spent 42 years of delving into many of the world's spiritual traditions from the age of thirty. I call myself a "scrutineer," trying to figure out what's true. I fix houses for a living, sort of a glorified handyman. I rarely work full time, valuing time more than money. So with time on my hands, I contemplate whatever I discover, following its trail until I'm satisfied. And I want to share some of that here.

And one of the things I noticed, among those I grew up with, was that people quoted Paul of Tarsus half the time. They seemed to be following Paul, not Jesus. Most Christians seem to be Paulists. Worst still, some say the Christian religion has become a religion 'about' Jesus, not Jesus' religion. For instance, he was first of all part of the Jewish tradition, so why do Christians eat pork? I'm sure Jesus never did. Should we follow his example or what Paul says?

It is said that God told Moses and Muhammad to tell the people we shouldn't eat pork. Jesus' example would have been enough for his followers, most of whom were Jews. They knew the food laws.

So why the pig? For people living in towns and villages it is a very useful creature to keep for cleaning up waste near their dwellings. But then I guess famine would strike and they would eat the pigs, and afterward, they just kept eating them.

And then think of this: the flu virus comes from Asia annually where millions of people live close to their pigs. Viruses jump back and forth between people and pigs, mutating and spreading worldwide, killing hundreds of thousands, and keeping me in bed for a week once!

Is that possibly one reason not to proliferate this animal? If Christians had followed God's instructions, maybe there would be just a few pigs in zoos today. I think it was Paul who changed that prohibition on pork, just to get the numbers up.

In the story of Jesus exorcising a man with demons, he throws the demons from the man into the pigs. Now the Christians go and eat the pigs. Maybe Teacher is sending us a message?

I had a spiritual teacher in my thirties for six years. Well, I'm still digesting what he taught me. And he said that Jesus would not enter a house where pork was served. I guess there were a lot of non-Jews around at the time.

We called my teacher, Bawa Muhaiyaddeen. Bawa means Father; Muhaiyaddeen was an honorary title approximating "reviver of the light of wisdom." What was his religion? I always saw him as a universal person because he could speak to any tradition, and had students from every tradition. But people understood that he was mainly coming from the Sufi tradition. But there aren't many Sufis who know what he knows or taught in his way.

Sufi, isn't that something to do with Islam? Some of you have heard of the 13th century Sufi poet, Rumi. One of the most popular poets in America today! It is the mystical tradition of Islam, like the Gnostics of Christianity, or the Hasidim of Judaism, or the Gnana (wisdom) yoga of Hinduism.

3

Six years with an enlightened being

My mother was a Methodist, and Dad an agnostic. So I went to church in the neighborhood until I was about twelve. Then I started to see through some of the things they were saying, and no one could answer my questions: not my Dad, not the church minister. My Mum just had pure faith, but I needed explanations. It's funny, I can't remember the day someone told me that Jesus was crucified, but I bet it was a bit traumatizing. Now that I think of it, they probably followed real quick with the "he died for your sins" theory. Oh that's good. So I'm culpable for his death?

I think Paul made this up, a kind of historical revisionism, to help his mind deal with the cruelty of a crucifixion. That never worked for me because if he died for my sins, that meant I could do whatever I wanted in life, and it didn't matter because Jesus got my back! Doesn't that remove my responsibility?

And I saw a fair bit of suffering around me growing up working class in England in the 1950s. So, I thought, "Why go through all this stuff? I might as well commit suicide and avoid it all. After all, Jesus died for my sins – he can cover me on that one too!" I was not suicidal and didn't tell anyone of my thought process. But the above didn't ring true either.

Even on the television, there was never discussion of the purpose of human existence. Television was less trivial back then. You'd think this question was so important to humans that we would be discussing it all the time, but there was no sign of it. So, being young, I decided my religion would be "just have a good time." Why not?

Now I see the wisdom of the parables of Jesus was always in the background of my life. And so it was until I met Bawa Muhaiyaddeen, and while listening to him, I realized I'd found the Explainer. All the questions I'd bagged up for Jesus, or whomever, he had the answers to it all. He never even hesitated to answer or call me a nuisance like so many others. His answers were so complete, and he was so giving that I soon moved into the house where he lived. The community who gathered about him bought it as a center where he could share his wisdom.

He was very old when we met, always saying that his time was soon up and that God had granted him an extension. So I got six years with who I considered to be the wisest person in the world before he died in 1986. For the first time in my life, I was grateful that I was no one, with no significant life position, title, or career to abandon, free to join him. I saw many who had that and could only visit from time to time.

The community also purchased land to serve as a cemetery for its members, and we buried him there in the way he had instructed us. No embalming, no coffin, we wrapped him in a shroud, lying on the earth, with boards over his body, supported by an earthen ledge. When we shoveled in the soil, it landed on the boards, not the body. He said the body came from the earth, so it should return there. We try to bury the dead within twenty-four hours.

Those six years enabled me to be in personal contact with Bawa almost daily. He was not like some royal figure who only appeared occasionally. His room was accessible to house residents for two thirds of the day. Visitors came at all times of the day to ask his advice. They asked questions from, "How do I fix my back, to who is God?" And unless he was not feeling well, he would serve the people. Even after visitors left, or things quieted down, he would ask, "What shall we do now?" These moments often led to a group cooking session.

Enlightened people are very rare. Many teachers have deep knowledge of their religious tradition. But to be enlightened, you must have transcended the monkey mind, (more on that later), brought your ego to extinction, and be in the very presence of God. I witnessed that.

Sometimes I would approach him with a question about building maintenance. Before I could ask, he would say, "Yes, just do that."

I'd say, "I was thinking of fixing the gates."

"Yes, yes, go ahead, but buy new material."

This kind of exchange happened more than once. There was no question he knew our thoughts, even our whole life experience. We all witnessed these things very often. A realized being is rare. They are selfless. With the students who say they've committed to the teachings the teacher must also be firm sometimes but are never cruel. Those who gathered around Bawa intended to self-improve to the highest level, which I understand is the point of human existence.

To be genuinely engaged in our religions, it's not enough to shout slogans about them and have the identity of belonging to a community. Or to create your own "impostor" religion or make a prophet in your own image!

There must be a character improvement component for the true adherent. What I call "The Know Thyself Curriculum." This study appears to be missing from much religious education. So I'll share the curriculum that Bawa showed me as I understand it.

And through this intimate relationship with him, I saw how a true spiritual guide conducted his affairs and advised those around him. He had virtually no time to himself, accepted no payment, and modeled the behavior of a genuine holy person – which can only be done by someone who has fully embraced the qualities of God.

4

Jesus and Mary ponder what to do

I imagine that when Paul of Tarsus shows up as a Christian persecutor in the Jerusalem area – about a year after the crucifixion – and after his self-reported super-natural encounter with Jesus on the road to Damascus, not many would want to talk with him about Jesus. Why would they? Dangerous times. Only yesterday he was persecuting followers of Jesus. No one ever talks about who sponsors him to do this. How do they feel about him now that he has supposedly converted to the other side? No repercussions for him? Even if he met disciples who knew that Judas was crucified and not Jesus, they wouldn't let on, because then Paul's question would be, where is he? So, those in the know would have no incentive to reveal what happened, thereby protecting Jesus, wherever he was.

According to Paul's writings, (Galatians 1:16-20), he believes he's had personal instruction from Jesus during his road-to-Damascus experience, and doesn't even need to confer with the disciples to hear about Jesus' life's work and teachings. Please! Now I hear people, who never met my teacher, Bawa (Father,

Teacher), lecturing about what he was like. Frankly, they have no idea. And so Paul sets off on his various marketing campaigns, coming up with whatever he needs to get the largest crowd into the tent and satisfy the gaps in his understanding.

But this begs the question, where would Jesus and Mary decide to go? Let's remember the early years of their lives, of which we know nothing. Where were they then? Historians have said that the census, that's supposed to take Mary and Joseph to Bethlehem, was probably an invention by the person who wrote the gospel of Mathew (way after the destruction of the temple in Jerusalem in 70 AD) to justify an Old Testament prophecy that a messiah would be born there. Only two the gospels of Mathew and Luke have the nativity story.

Professor Bart D. Ehrman in Jesus, Interrupted, alerts us that this would be an impossible thing to ask of the whole population back then or even today. Imagine stopping their lives, abandoning their homes, land, crops and animals. Then somehow funding such an expedition and finding transport either donkey or camel, or walking to their ancestral birthplaces along dangerous highways with children or pregnant, carrying enough supplies to get you there and back. And then, I'm thinking, to hold up in a stinky barn full of animal dung, flies, possibly rats and snakes. What a stink! They would have been better off camping in the sand dunes, or an olive orchard, along with others who could help them; if any of that happened.

According to the Koran recited about 550 years later by Prophet Muhammad, yes, Muslims revere Jesus also, in the chapter titled Mary, verse 23: "And the pangs of childbirth drove her unto the trunk of a palm tree." This account is more sobering.

Nevertheless, I acknowledge they may have been in danger from some evil administrator, possibly more than once, and so would others, and have to flee the area of Galilee or Jerusalem. It could be that Joseph, with his travel experience and knowledge of the region, knew of a better place to raise Jesus than the Roman dominated, political boiling pot of the Jerusalem of that day. Jesus and Mary, having years of familiarity with that place, might decide to return there. They would be safer there because people know them and could continue fully being who they are.

Notice I said "they." Mary is also extraordinary, being in a highly divine state. I don't think she's a shrinking violet, an ordinary village woman. To give birth to a prophet of Jesus' caliber, you have to be in a pure state with little or no karma (more on karma later). This state of consciousness is not the accident of innocence. It is an intentional state of being arising from a family that understands such things – an inheritance from family members who consciously practiced spiritual growth. Such a condition is not nepotism, but divine meritocracy. It does not occur to nations or tribes, but only at the individual family level.

Historian, Arnold J. Toynbee, was onto this. "In each of these civilizations, mankind, I think, is trying to rise above mere humanity – above primitive humanity, that is – towards some higher kind of spiritual life. One cannot predict the goal because it has never been reached – or, rather, I should say that it has never been reached by any human society. It has, perhaps, been reached by individual men and women. At least, I can think of certain saints and sages who seem to me, in their personal lives, to have reached the goal, at least in so far as I myself am able to conceive what the goal may be like. But if there have been a few transfigured men and women, there has never been such a thing as a civilized society…There has never been a communion of saints on earth." (P. 55, Civilization on Trial).

This transfigured state Toynbee refers to is called Man – God, God – Man in Hinduism, Insan Kamil: Perfected Man in Arabic, or True Man; Man, of course, meaning the zenith of the human state, not gender-based. If I use it, it is for this exalted meaning; otherwise we are men and women, male or female.

You can imagine in this scenario that during Mary and Jesus' decision-making time about where to go, various disciples meet up with Jesus, and he invites them to come along with them. This could be fodder for the Gospel narratives of seeing Jesus, so-called, physically risen from the dead. But, when you consider Jesus' exalted spiritual state, internally merged with God, in a state of non-duality, there is no need for such a person to be reborn. He is already in a state of enlightenment, not separate from God as most of us are. God's pre-installed software (the original GPS) is within us, and we can reach the same state. But few will attain it, being more in love with the world and one's illusory existence!

And that leads to the statement supposedly made by Jesus on the cross, "Why hast Thou forsaken me?" I don't think Jesus would ever say such a thing. This is the statement of an ordinary person. I'm not yet enlightened; still working on it, but I wouldn't utter those words at this stage in my life and inner work. I fully know that God is the only reality, within and without me, aware of my meager existence so that I couldn't utter such a faithless thing, and nor would Jesus. But someone in Judas' mental state would. Could anyone get close enough to hear and record it?

It's hard to leave your hometown, family, and life. We've seen how wrenching that is for migrants and people even fleeing oppression. In the end, I could imagine no one wants to leave their family home, and so we'll have Jesus and Mary leave Jerusalem alone.

5

Jesus and Mary leave Jerusalem

In the Gospel narratives, where it's mentioned, Mary, Joseph and the baby Jesus, supposedly head into Egypt after the birth. But why would they go to the same place Moses and his people were said to have escaped from about 1,250 years before? That's if the Exodus ever happened, which I think it did, just not the way it's reported. But besides even that, it's a fully fascist country full of idol worshipers with super-strange burial rites, wall-to-wall enslaved people, and unjust social structures! Quite normal for so many "human" settlements in those days. So I don't think that's the place. No, I think it's somewhere more conducive. I'll give you a hint.

The story goes that Moses led the people out of Egypt, trying to get to what is Israel today, the so-called Promised Land, but couldn't due to foreigners preventing them. And so it is said that they hung around Sinai for 40 years until it was possible. They're within a day's bus ride of the Promised Land and they wait for 40 years before they decide to hike it? This is the part that falls apart for me. Either the 40 years is an exaggeration, or they take the long route. And what would that be?

I see them turn right at Sinai and wander down south into today's Arabia. (Which, by the way, has approximately the same area as India! It's a big place.) Then continuing all the way down to Yemen, turning left along that south coast, then left again – there's no choice really. The Arabian sea surrounds it, which is also the northern Indian Ocean. Then they travel north again, following the east coast, through what is today, Oman, United Arab Emirates, Kuwait, etc., and up through Mesopotamia, today's Iraq, through today's Syria and in the back door to the Promised Land.

It would probably take that long for Moses to distill the idol worship out of his people that they absorbed from Egyptian culture. Meanwhile, almost every other people in the area and the world were idol worshipers back then. I should think with age attrition and a whole new generation, most of those who end the Exodus trek weren't those who began it. I also think that along the way, some may have said, "To heaven with this Promised Land trek. We like it right here. You go on; we're staying put." I probably would have been one of those. In fact, the scant known history of Arabia shows that there were tribes of Israel related people living in various enclaves throughout the region in ancient times (Arabia and the Arabs – author: Robert G. Hoyland and other works).

Let us not forget that it is believed Jesus moved

around the Jerusalem region, working his mission, for only about 3 years. Therefore, he could have been in his childhood location until that time. So it would have been only about 3 years since he took that journey, and now I have him returning on that same route.

I want to send them off to Petra first. It's the ancient rock city some people are familiar with, located in today's Jordan, also called wadi Musa (Moses' oasis). It was a well-worn route and crossroads back then for walking travelers and camel and donkey trekkers. At Petra, one would check with all the caravans encamped there to find the suitable one for the continuing journey. This was a main travel hub on the ancient Nabatean trade routes that came north from Yemen, selling frankincense, myrrh and goods imported to the southern shores from India and the Far East. Surprisingly, although not far from Jerusalem, there was not much Roman influence at that time.

And following that trade route, Mary and Jesus would find their caravan, then set off south with their sites set on Yathrib, where I believe they spent the missing early years. It was far from Roman influence and the Jewish religious hierarchy of Jerusalem, which would probably be threatened by Jesus' message, just as most religious establishments are when a prophet arrives in their midst – a threat to their job security!

It would probably take several weeks to get there by caravan in those days. Can't find Yathrib on the map? Today it is called Medina in Saudi Arabia. We know there was a large Jewish community (People of the book) living there in the time of Muhammad (approx. 600 CE.) as recorded in the Koran. Jesus and Mary would have fitted in fine there: language, customs, One-God focus, social support, although there would also be many idol-worshiping Arabians in the neighborhoods.

I've come to believe that all prophets and holy personages are universal people, not attached to any national identity. They didn't come to share the revelations with just one people, but all humans on earth. Of course, they are born amongst certain people and use their language, but that's because they have bodies too! But back then, it would have been very difficult for Jesus and Mary to live exclusively among polytheists with their understanding of God. They would have incurred the troubles of Muhammad, but that wasn't part of their mission, it would be his when he arrived in 570 CE.

Jesus and Mary would have been able to live modestly among the Jews of Medina. Jesus, working as a carpenter with the contacts he already had if that's where he grew up and was a carpenter. He would obviously have been an inspiration to anyone he shared spiritual insights with, possibly drawing a dedicated group around him, even from among people of different religions.

We should also remember the presence of the Ishmaelites – Abraham's family descended through an Egyptian woman, Hagar – who populated the area. Those of whom hadn't fallen into idol worship, like the few the close followers of Moses who accepted Yahweh, the One un-created God, (whom the Ishmaelites called Allah), would have recognized the wisdom of Jesus and possibly would be among his companions in Medina.

That's a very exciting prospect for me. If Jesus could have lived out his life there, it would have been sufficient time to influence a large group of people to keep the faith, no matter what. And who knows, inspire the families in spiritual devotion sufficiently to produce another prophet centuries later. None of those people would have seen it as a new religion, just further revelation from God. I've personally come to understand that the monotheistic tradition from Adam to Muhammad is just one tradition and not separate religions. God doesn't do separate religions. There is One God, one family of humans and one continuing revelation sent by God and brought by the lights of God! This goes for all humanity because God sends his wise ones to all the peoples of the Earth.

So, in Medina, we actually have two monotheistic communities: the Jews through Isaac (Abraham's Family through Sarah,) and the Ishmaelites through Ishmael (Abraham's Family thru Hagar), both born to Abraham. Besides the very spiritual families who hadn't lost their faith, idol worshipers were in both camps for many centuries.

According to recent archeology (Finkelstein and Silberman's research), they found idols in the rubble of Israeli homes in today's Israel region up until about 500 BCE. Then suddenly, that stops with the return to Jerusalem of Jewish exiles from Babylon who were carrying the Torah, thought now to be compiled in its most complete written form. The power of the written word? Probably the same didn't occur for the majority of people in the Arabian Peninsula until after prophet Muhammad revealed the Koran in the mid-seventh century CE, and soon after written down.

6

Introducing the
"know thyself curriculum"

Now, if Jesus was about 33 years old, as is believed, around the time of Judas's crucifixion, Mary was probably in her early 50s, that's quite old for that time. So, depending on different factors, she could be ailing with advancing age or living much longer with good health due to her innate wisdom.

(Does wisdom improve health, leading to healthier, longer life? I can emphatically say, yes! If you have wise judgment, you won't over-eat. You will have reasoned that corporate processed foods do not contain the nutrients necessary for human life and so you will eat mainly whole, natural foods.

Bawa told us in 1986 that food in the future would be forbidden to us, so we often had daily communal cooking session with him as he explained the process that guides my cooking routine till this day. Yep, you have to cook your own if you want the best! You won't imbibe intoxicants. You won't engage in extreme behavior. You will be more centered and in control of your emotions, and understand the world more clearly – even the most ridiculous things happening around you and the larger world.)

In that case, I could see that with her God-serving heart, Mary might have a mission of her own to complete, in addition to being the mother of Jesus. With ships coming to the Arabian coastline from far-off lands, they would hear about all kinds of places where the 'Word' had not arrived, or where the people ignored it, like so many places and people.

Mary may have heard of a specific place where her presence could make a difference and been moved to travel there, possibly never returning to her ancestral land. When I was in northern Sri Lanka, local people showed me a gravesite they thought to be Mary's last resting place! And in other parts of the world, there are legends of the burial places of biblical holy personages.

You can imagine that wherever Jesus grew up, he would have followers because prophets are born in the presence of God and don't lose it like we did. So from fifteen to thirty years old, he would have been sharing divine inspiration with those in his community. Because of my own experience with Bawa, I think Jesus would have dispensed more in-depth teachings with his closest companions before and during the Jerusalem period (and after, if there was such a time). He would have shared through teaching stories, parables and "The Know Thyself Curriculum."

This curriculum comes through the writings of the "wisdom traditions" of the Far East: the Hindu Epics, Buddhism, and Taoism. It appears to me the monotheistic texts didn't explicitly include them. But I experienced it through my close association with Bawa Muhaiyaddeen, and I feel duty-bound to share that now.

I also feel it is absolutely essential to introduce this "Know Thyself" teaching to sincere monotheistic students without delay to elevate the awareness of those adherents to live above mere religious belonging, slogans, and unexamined dogma. It boggles the mind that Jews, Christians and Muslims fight each other when they are part of the same religious heritage. Bawa said that people fight wars for land, women and gold with rare exceptions. It is not the peasantry, the welder or the nurse who start these wars. It is the wealthy 1%. They use whatever deceptions they can to further their aims, including religion, which continues glaringly into the present.

Mind, Brain, and Soul.

Let us consider the mind, brain, and soul. These words are sometimes used interchangeably and loosely in common parlance, but I've got to tie them down and be more accurate. From my understanding, the human mind is an ideational projection from the elements within the body toward and from the elements in the world. The brain is not the mind. The brain is hardwired for some bodily functions, but it also receives, stores and processes this ideational projection communicating it to others. The mind only understands physicalism. And it is constantly at war with the idea of uncreated existence and intelligence because it doesn't understand formlessness, just as ignorant people won't research what you say about a complex subject, but only react on a narrow, pre-programmed emotional level.

Actually, "The mind is the distance between a human and God," Bawa used to say. He also used to say, "Religion is shit." That is surprising coming from the most spiritual person I ever met. But that's because religion is the mind's attempt at worshipping God. Which pretty much guarantees you won't actually succeed at getting to really know this God. Which is fine with the mind, because it really does have a mind of its own, wanting to protect its ephemeral existence.

Gustav Jung realizing this says, "Religion is a defense against the experience of God." Wow! And how did religion become so degraded because the 1%, who really believe in wealth, power and the world, took it over long ago? The mind will tell you it is moral so that you won't attempt any kind of self-knowledge work or purification. That's the beginning of the end of the mind, or at least its curtailment, just leaving it the bits that it handles best, the worldly stuff. But the mind wants your whole life, the eternal part as well. To be or not to be, what? To be the mind and not the soul, or to be the soul and not the mind, what is the answer?

The soul also uses the brain to communicate with this world. The mind can wire the brain, or the soul can. The ideational projection, called the mind, is not an objective observer because everything it sees is through the veil of karma. What is karma? Your inherited and made-up ideas of what you think you see filtered through your race, religion, self image, age, time in history, family moral basis, your personal desires, your needs and wants…on and on. Now does that sound like we're objectively observing reality? Or is all reality subjective anyway? In which case, let's do away with the word reality and just call it subjectality!

For the soul to get a chance to observe, it's a bit like having learnt which room contains the electron beam microscope. But it's not enough to know the room number to access it. You must be trained to use it. If you've studied in a university that doesn't have an electron beam microscope or a country that has never heard of such a thing, then you won't be familiar with it. In other words, if the soul was not accurately nurtured in you from childhood, you only know how to use the mind and you only believe in the world, not a formless eternity.

So, there is the brain – which communicates with the world; the mind – let's call it attitudinal observation and processing; and the soul, which is God's point of view, and in my opinion, the only objective observation. Most of us actually look through this with the attachment called the mind, like putting a veil over the lens of the electron beam microscope. And most of us have very minimal training in how to use it, which should be the work of religion. So, where does all this lead us? Indulge me in this imagining as an illustration.

An Illustration.

Let's say your family were of European descent from America, and your parents were missionaries sent to China when you were six months old. They brought you with them, and the car you traveled in went off the mountain road and burst into flames. Your parents were both incinerated in the accident, as was most of the car, but you were thrown clear and landed in a soft reed bed near a stream (come on, these things happen). The locals arrive at the scene, buried your parents and disposed of the car parts. They took you in and raised you. Because this was in the back-of-beyond, no one outside the village knew about it.

You would grow up thinking you were that village's tall Chinese girl or boy. You would speak their language, eat their food, have preference for that food, fall in love with someone in that village, find a working niche there and maybe become a parent yourself.

So, we all think we are who we are, but we are products of our environment. Years later, if someone arrives in that village and tells you that you are an American, you will laugh, and so will those around you who didn't know your story. If that person said you're coming with me to America where you'll never need to grow or cook your own food again. You're going to eat industrial processed food and warm it up in a microwave oven. You'll become overweight or obese, maybe get diabetes. You'll own a car and drive ninety minutes a day to and from work, and work 60 hours a week, and... You might not want to go!

So who are we? Who are we really when you take away all the karma? If this God exists, who or what did It intend you to be? Who or what are you now? Who or what is looking through these eyes? Who or what should be your self-image? "Thinking," Bawa used to say, "is the elements arguing with each other," or, in modern terms, chemicals spitting at each other across synaptic gaps. And then he would say, "And what you call your life, is your character's dream of those thoughts."

So I ask you for an honest reply: How are we going to get around the mind and karma to know our authentic self and thereby, from that position, truly worship the One Omnipresent, Omniscient, Omnipotent God? By going to church, mosque or synagogue once a week? We need to develop some digging tools to go deeper.

7

Digging Deeper

Going deeper then entails seeing ourselves and making appropriate changes. 'What do I need to change? Are you saying I'm not the model of a human being?' You couldn't get away with much in the working class street where I grew up. "Who do you think you are?" was a common refrain? Any attitude or haughtiness got cut with the precision of a Samurai sword. Isn't it amazing how we can always see other people's crap and not our own?

I found this great exchange in Twelfth Night, by Shakespeare that speaks to this:

Duke: I know thee well. How dost thou, my good fellow?

Fool: Truly, sir, the better for my foes, and the worse for my friends.

Duke: Just the contrary: the better for thy friends.

Fool: No, sir, the worse.

Duke: How can that be?

Fool: Sir, my friends praise me and make an ass of me. Now my foes tell me plainly that I am an ass; so that by my foes, sir, I profit in knowledge of myself, and

> by my friends I am abused; why then, the worse for
> my friends, and the better for my foes.
> Duke: Why, this is excellent.

Here we have the solution to a conundrum I could never understand. Why did so many thousands of people visit Teacher, but few stay. Maybe Joseph Campbell can answer that for us from the Power of Myth: "It's a terrifying experience to have your consciousness transformed… People are not psychologically prepared for spiritual transformation." A failure once again of mainstream religion – "Don't give them anything to do that's difficult; we want the pews filled!" Paul of Tarsus' legacy, methinks!

Not a sky god.

And so wisdom-beings come into the world explaining, "You are not the modern beings you think you are, with these titles and ideas of yourself. You are actually soul beings, true children of God." And they don't mean it in a nicey, nicey churchy way, but rather, we have immortal souls that can know what God knows. The purpose and duration of our lives to be always advancing towards Man-God, God-Man. This aim is concurrent with our lives as music stars, lawyers, accountants, plumbers, CEOs, carpenters, nurses or midwives – and all other efforts to feed the stomach.

Real wisdom-beings spend every waking second

showing us the path to achieve this. It is within our reach. Maybe that is what Jesus meant in the testament of John 14:12, where they reported he said: "Truly, truly, I say to you, he who believes in Me, the works that I do, he will do also; and greater works than these he will do; because I go to the Father." I conclude that we were born for this more than any other reason.

I submit this piece to dispel fears that I'm talking about the sky god that I was raised on as a kid. Remembered by me when a person asked Bawa, "How should God and politics come together in the public arena?"

He answered, "God is a power that pervades everything, everywhere. It is mingled within our bodies and souls. Is there anything like the Father and Mother who is God, anything like It on this Earth? The One mingled within love within us since the eternal beginning. The One who is the food of love, the happiness of Grace. As friend and relative of love, this God who is within us, who exists and rules the center of our hearts. Where can we find an equal to That? Where can we find something similar to God who is the Mother of our souls? He who is the lucidity of wisdom."

At this point the questioner, believing Teacher has misunderstood the question, tries to jump in. But Teacher lifts his hand gently and continues, "This flower that radiates the Grace of divine wisdom has no form and is uncreated and yet exists everywhere.

Is there any such thing as this on Earth? One who performs knowing the mind of all creations, the great effulgence that existed before, now and forever. The One who is the form of kindness and generosity within Grace. Who is the form beyond form of patience and tolerance within forbearance. Is there any such One in this universe? It is compassion, perfection, happiness, the open space beyond all imagination and spectacle. The fruit of the heart, contained within as truth within truth, as the soul within the soul, as wisdom within wisdom. Resplending as grace within grace, as the grace that shines everywhere, as the radiant flame becoming divine light, and that formless Thing which becomes God - is the thing that is God. That which exists as love within love, is God. And everything else, my brother, is politics."

Now I'm sitting there with my heart-center reso-nating with this description and I'm comparing it to that mean god described in the Old Testament that I was raised on, thinking, yeah, that's right. Where did that mean god come from? Oh! Wait a minute. I bet some one-percenters wrote that in, kind of creating a god in their own image so they could justify their cruelty.

Years later I read in The Power of Myth by Joseph Campbell, "If your guiding divinity is brutal, your decisions will be brutal." Is that why the Christians start so many wars? Is that why our schoolteachers beat us back in the 1950s and 60s? I always wanted to

ask the ones who professed to be followers of Jesus
if they thought Jesus would have beaten the children,
but my father had disempowered me to toe the line,
I realize now. Even if a teacher hit me, I didn't go
home and tell my parents because in all likelihood,
my father would just say, "You must have deserved
it." After all, he had a leather belt hanging on the door
with the threat that if you stepped too far out of line, it
would end up across your ass. But I never remember
him using it.

Jesus said, "Love your enemies," were we children
worse than enemies? The Koran also has its share
of God's punishment, although it's often followed
by, "Except those who speak my name and do good
works." And every chapter begins with, "In the name
of God the most merciful and compassionate," which
Teacher asked us to say before any action. Many modern people (mainly males) of that tradition seem to
have overlooked these words as they act brutally.

Throwing God into the sky.

At thirty years old, why hadn't I realized that God
might be something more like Teacher described?
With his student's help, Teacher used to make artis-
tic renderings. The title of one work was The Rocky
Mountain of the Heart, explaining that some people's
hearts are harder than stone. The density of our karma
may be to blame. We'll explore that next. From about

5,000 years ago, once the city-state had us grouping in large numbers of people, there were always those who wanted to rule over others. They were usually the most aggressive, not the most intelligent or worthy. That's still ongoing today. Then there are oppression and warring factors against other city-states. And the oppressors always want the other group's wealth, forcing us to fight for "land, women and gold."

This God that Teacher described spoke to my innate kindness. How did It end up in the sky, behind a cloud, with a weapon waiting to hit us if we stepped out of line? And don't forget, "the wages of sin is death," Romans 6:23. These are Paul's words, not Jesus'. After Bawa died, I took it upon myself to do some reading, the kind you get in a college education, the Classics. While reading the Greek myths, that it dawned on me this plethora of sky gods, which has so enamored the academy (universities) for 2,000 years, is the influence that threw our monotheistic, formless, omnipresent God into the sky. Then, throughout time, because the 1% took over the religions, Jesus gets bedecked in silk robes and often a crown studded with gems, creating a Jesus in their 1% image. And there you have it. No longer a non-materialistic prophet, humble, full of compassion, wisdom beyond imagining, champion of everybody – but a king!

And even while Jesus was alive, he was done a disservice by calling him the king of Israel, jeopardizing his life because the 1% felt threatened by a usurper. The 1% always feel threatened because they have so much material wealth or power to lose. There is indeed some wisdom in the Greek myths. But the idolatry is a disservice to the truth, always threatening to overthrow Yahweh, Allah, Andavan – one God – uncreated Power of the universe. Let's reclaim the great effulgence within us that existed before, now and forever, unchaining It from religion's shackles.

8

On Karma

The period of Jesus' life between the ages of fifteen to thirty was a bounteous time to share divine knowledge. If these numbers are to be believed, it would be five times the duration he spent on the Jerusalem part of his mission.

From what I've experienced of the spiritual path, those who take it on go through a "great sorting." Distinguishing the mind from the soul and understanding the role of the brain, then realizing and accepting that everyone has karma, which is literally: the ethical, moral and physical consequences of thoughts and actions.

Here is my distillation of years of study about karma. I mainly use the word as a negative because the soul has no karma. There appear to be five significant contributors to karma:

1) The inheritance at the time of conception - totality of mother and father's wisdom and ignorance.

2) The influence of parents after birth.

3) The influence of society, relatives, culture, education, schoolteachers.

4) The effect of misunderstandings and misperceptions.

5) The illusions of the adult mind compounded from the previous four.

Let's explore these a little.

The inheritance at the time of conception – totality of mother and father's wisdom and ignorance:

We would probably say that this is genetic. Bawa said it came with the blood. He called them "blood-ties," which many took to be blood relations, and in many cases, this was true. But I think this was his phrase for "biology." Because he also said there is no karma in the soul. The soul has no dark side. The soul, here defined, is pure, a spark of God. My definition of Man merging with God's soul within us is that the soul is a piece of God. There can't be my soul and God. They must be one. But karma and illusion are so pervasive they seem to invade every part of us. But they don't. No matter what happens the soul is always there in its perfection. The work of ceasing the mind and merging with the soul is what we're about. I know we say, "It hurt my soul," but I think that is the soul discerning the violation of goodness, fair-play, or justice; but the soul isn't corrupted, and it's not a created object like the brain. It's just that the mind surrounds it, sort of.

The influence of parents after birth:

Once born, our parents or guardians' karma transfers to us. They tell us our race and religion. They transfer their prejudices, likes, and dislikes. We become attached to a certain culture seeing ourselves as different from the rest of the world family. They give us their fears, history, level of self-esteem, expectations, and passions. They also give us their good qualities, level of generosity, and kindness. But it's a mixed bag, often contingent on karmic influences, and it's this we'll have to sort throughout our whole life.

The influence of society, relatives, culture, education, schoolteachers:

As we grow older, the society and culture around us will have their influence, whether we live in central Africa or the USA, they may be negative or positive. Various relatives and family friends will command our attention, and we will inherit things from them. Then we will be subjected to the education system of the day and the teachers who teach it. Most of this education will revolve around the physical world and one or two people's view of history and told through the veil of their karma.

If God's story is taught at all, it will be a devolved version of the original prophetic message. A version sanctioned through the karma of religious hierarchies of past and present. We are all living this!

The effect of misunderstandings and misperceptions:

None of us knows what the other is thinking. I've probed folks over my lifetime, and we all give different meaning to the things life presents, especially, I think, those with mental illness. And if some of the important things in life are misunderstood or misperceived, then what life throws at us will only confuse. Which in extreme cases may lead to minor or major pathologies and irrational behavior.

The illusions of the adult mind compounded from the previous four:

In adulthood, Teacher said, "Illusion teaches us." If you accept the transient foundation of the first four, it isn't difficult to see that our adult perception will probably be flawed or at best inaccurate. Most of this results in us believing in the world. Because we are unaware of just how corrupted our journey has been so far, it is no wonder that some of us have no idea what is happening.

Two of my favorite phrases as a kid were, "what's it all about?" and, "why are we here?" Now I know why those around me couldn't answer my questions. If any of them ever asked these questions, they had forgotten them long ago and got on with the business of survival. When you grow up seeing soap operas on television mimicking parts of the life you see around you daily, it's hard to believe that everyone has got it wrong. But now I believe this is so. I want to walk onto these TV drama sets and say to camera, "Hey kids, this isn't reality, they're lying to you, they made up some ideas about what human beings are and it's all untrue. What they're showing you are the animal-men and women, don't fall for it, become "karma-busters," make it real. You're so much more exalted than this!"

So for many of us, our first story is literally our parents' story. We have to edit that story and sift it, keeping only what's good while adding as much wisdom as possible as we go on the path of life. You may have looked inside on occasions and asked, "Where did that come from?" Well, now you know. You may have inherited it.

Incidentally, those who think they were someone long ago in a past life were probably not. Some memory of this may have been passed to you many generations ago. Very few people have been born before. You don't want to be in your second birth. Bawa insisted that this birth is the best one to get this 'work' done. If there is such a thing as reincarnation, you would be disempowered each time, eventually becoming an animal. Also, consider that we change every time we have a new thought. Are we a new person? Does it depend on how much that thought reshaped us?

9

Adam and Eve

At the latest count, experts believe Homo sapiens (self-named wise hominids!) have been around about 200,000 years. That's a lot of time to gather some inter-generational karma and start behaving more like homo ignorami! And then, only about 50,000 years ago, figurines began showing up in the archeological record that may represent some kind of sacred idol figure. In other words, our distant ancestors are having supernatural thoughts, possibly inventing idol worship, sensing something mysterious in their existence. And boy, does it take off. Looking at the last 15,000 years, we've all seen in the history documentaries that worship of objects made of earth materials takes hold in myriad forms among thousands of different cultures everywhere and even continues to this day in some places!

So here's my musing. What if Adam and Eve really were born about 5,700 years ago, as the Jewish biblical calendar suggests? Is there any way this could be true? I think so. But for this to happen we must de-couple the beginning of creation with their birth. We know, and I accept, that the fossil record shows the Earth and universe to be billions of years old. But, think back before 6,000 years. From the fossil record, we know that there were other kinds of humans: Australopithecus, Homo Erectus, Homo Habilis, Neanderthalensis, Denisovians, etc., and perhaps they had some of our higher cognition.

All of these subsequent human types have died out in their pure form, but I always thought that some of their genes could be mixed in with those alive today. And in fact, we now know, through DNA testing, that there is a small percentage of Neanderthal in most Caucasian people today. But, by 6,000 or so years ago, Homo Sapiens is the predominant species of humans and possibly the only one. Also, looking at the Earth at that time, we would see millions of people all over the planet. Experts say only about 5 million, seems small, but I accept that.

But what was their inner state of consciousness? Can you trust them? Would you want to be in their company? I wonder. Even today there are some very unsavory people around who many of us wouldn't want to have coffee, even though some of them are socially elevated and have prestigious titles. But one's social status or wealth doesn't guarantee an exalted inner or spiritual state. No. As I've been discussing, we must earn an elevated spiritual state through inner work.

What if, from among these millions of people wandering around 5,700 years ago, there were a few in an elevated, let's say, enlightened state of being. From what I've seen of "decent" people in my life, it runs in families, with few exceptions. In other words, over the generations, family members have been interested in ethical, spiritual and moral lifestyles, either consciously or not. Could this finally produce a person who can reach enlightenment? Is this its prerequisite? It's hard to overcome gross karmic behavior and reach this state in a lifetime without dedication and mentors who consciously understand this condition.

So I put it to you that a couple of families 5,700 years ago managed to produce an exalted archetypal being that I'll call Adam. And because he wouldn't be able to tolerate a partner with gross behavior, he found an exalted female we can call Eve with whom to spend his life and reproduce. Does that mean all the people alive today are descended from this couple? Probably not. Does that mean some are descended from the rest? Did the rest slowly become more exalted (human) over the years, kind of catching up? Or not? This could explain some things. Maybe a few Adam and Eve beings were born in different human populations, isolated on various landmasses. And these are the best of human archetypes. Perhaps the descendants of these Adams of Eves began and continued the prophet lines throughout history, those we know of and the thousands we don't.

A prophetic lineage may sound like nepotism to some. Still, I would posit that the exalted states of the prophets don't happen by accident and that again this generational self-improvement is a prerequisite. And this is down to the extended family level, I believe. Therefore if a prophet is born within a national boundary, the nation cannot claim to be exalted, only that family. After all, all nations have their miscreants, some of them in leadership roles! To be a prophet, Bawa said, you must be capable of bringing the next chapter of revelation. So, under that definition, Buddha, for instance, wouldn't be a prophet because he studied the Hindu Vedanta and became exalted, Man-God, God-Man. This type of study is also the process of enlightenment that we, who are not prophets, must follow.

Therefore, I think Adam and Eve refer symbolically to the first humans capable of enlightenment. I could use the term "had evolved sufficiently to," but I don't think it is evolution because we are all born with this foundation and capability, but it is not nurtured. We must work consciously toward it, removing its opposite. This "the know thyself" curriculum aids this work.

This jump in consciousness from animal-human to perfected-human is so significant it would be an understatement to call it immense. And so, with this momentous occurrence, God's will of creating a creature capable of knowing Him, not imagining It, finally occurs. Adam is not only the first Man but the progenitor of the most recent prophet lineage in "recorded" history. When this prophet lineage speaks to human animals of the formless power of the universe, which is also creator, sustainer and protector of everything, it runs counter to their accustomed beliefs and behaviors. That is the plethora of religious objects (idols) and the mythologies invented to justify them.

It's hard for us in the modern world to imagine a leader of a country who actually believes or wants others to believe that they are a god. (Although recently, we may be witnessing a re-emergence of that!) Imagine the intolerance of such people toward those who do not agree with their every whim! They would have one of their henchmen execute them in the blink of an eye. We still have world leaders who are in this state of degradation and, if they rise to world prominence, will usher in a great destruction through their inhumanness. But these kinds of people were very prevalent amongst the leaders of old. Suppose one of them heard that a person had reached an enlightened state, with the understanding of monotheism, that only God is God. With fantasy religious structures in place, supported by bogus intricate cultural practices, it's not hard to see how prophets and truly wise people would be persecuted by the status quo where they lived.

In the tradition of the prophetic monotheistic message, Jesus' message of compassion, forgiveness, and worship of the One God, Yaweh, would challenge the fantasy gods of the Roman courts where even the Roman Emperors were fast becoming deified themselves.

So, to get a true prophet, first, you need a family who has had the thoughts: Are we just clever animals, or is there more? There appears to be another heart-centered awareness in me: is that anything? It seems to be a feeling of good, even informed by a moral sense. Suppose this awareness percolates for many generations, articulated by elders, shared with the young, developed as a way of life. In that case wisdom will become a large part of that community.

Using this wisdom, some community members examine their behavior sufficiently to reduce non-essential animal motivations while moving toward an understanding of higher human consciousness. Some children who can take it to a new level in their lives will inherit this higher consciousness. Eventually, birthing someone so consciously clear that they do not separate from God-consciousness as they grow.

By retaining that consciousness, they can genuinely share God's will with the rest of humanity. This state of being discussed here cannot be "appointed" to priests, ministers or even a pope. That is why the illumined ones rarely come through the religious hierarchy of the day, which is why they are often not accepted by the 1% religious or secular status quo or the society at large. They often have to address society's misdirection, resulting in the messengers being disparaged, instead of taking what they bring as helpful, honest feedback. (More on prophets later.)

10

But what is wisdom?

What is wisdom? Literally: Wise judgment. As understood here: The evolving ability to access objective reality, which for me is also God's point of view, consistently embodying compassion. Wisdom feeds insight and enhances our knowledge of self, helping us progress and gain clarity about life while eradicating the negatives. It is also knowledge of the unseen – divine knowledge.

Since adding a wisdom path to my life, I have identified other sources (see further reading) that I think are consistent with it. By bringing our life in line with this knowledge, we gain more of the "peace that passeth all understanding," moving closer to our true human potential. That doesn't mean our experiences will be the same, each one receives meaning according to their understanding. Those who are members of a religion would be surprised to discover what their fellow congregants believe. The truth is there are probably as many religions as there are people!

For me, wisdom is the process that can answer questions like: Why was I born? Did I exist before that? Will I exist after death? What is a human being? What are the animals? Who or what is God? What is the difference between mind, brain and soul (the inner, formless-heart)? What are all these spiritual traditions around the world? Is there a devil? What is illusion and what is real? Do I have to die? What is happiness and sadness? What is true justice? What is my true identity? Am I my body? Am I my mind? Why is there suffering? Where is God when the bad stuff happens? Which scripture or teaching is authentic? Ultimately, what is the purpose of human existence? What's it all about?

But, to answer these questions, we have to know something about ourselves. The more clarity we gain concerning human complexity, the more accurate we can answer these questions. Wisdom must be "applied," it cannot be just theoretical philosophy. Whatever we do, the world needs as many people as possible studying wisdom – becoming the light-beings that prevent darkness from overspreading. Were there any female prophets? I'm sure there were. But in ancient times a woman addressing an audience in the public arena was rare. Therefore, if we believe God sends prophets to declare guidance, it would be difficult for women to fulfill that role. But let's not forget that every prophet has a mother!

I no longer see separate religions within the monotheistic world. I have come to see the prophets as bringing chapters of God's story – the story revealed

But what is wisdom?

by God to humankind over thousands of years. With this in mind, I've tried to present here insights that can fit into all the traditions, stirring up their meaning and depth. Sometimes you may not like or be familiar with these explanations, and you may not feel that they apply to your tradition, but I have attempted to be as universal as possible. We may tend to be defensive, to quote the known familiar when new ideas challenge us. But if we are honest, many of us are not living the ideal. and we need to do some "work," have some self-honesty, and realize there is always room for some self-improvement. This tome assumes there is such a thing as an amazing, formless, creative, wise power called God. If you're an atheist or agnostic, I'm surprised you've got this far, but I believe the core-curriculum of developing self-knowledge can benefit us all.

11

About some prophets

So now the monotheistic prophet line has kicked off in the world with the descendants of Adam and Eves. The scriptural record shows us that much of the ancient world's population are discouraged from embracing their message for many different reasons, mainly because it's God's show, not the king or queens', the pharaohs' or the religious hierarchy.

Everyone is equal before God, the whole world population is one, despite language differences, appearance, wealth, or heritage.

God is rooted in love, mercy and compassion – a real blow to the warrior class. It takes faith to accept the invisible, formless God, and it is difficult for those with simple mind's that need a physical representation to grasp. Science can brainwash faith out of you. Today, some consider faith simplistic or even medieval. However, why was it easier to believe that the stone the craftsperson just carved into an idol should receive any devotional attention when the other half of the stone was installed as a step to enable us to walk up to the idol?

Of course, each tribe or nation had their personal gods, and these became part of the identity of that particular group, often upheld by the status quo. One day while explaining the message of a particular prophet, someone asked Bawa to describe the historical setting of that time. Bawa said, "I am not here to teach history. The history of the world is a murder story. I'm sharing with you the wisdom of the prophets. That's my role." So let me share with you some of that.

Bawa: "The story of God is in Man, and the story of Man is in God." We see eight prophets anchoring the present known monotheistic revelation. From these prophets, I've understood the story this way:

Father Adam is the "Chosen of God" and the one who chose. He chose truth. Likewise, we must follow the same trajectory to re-establish our divinity. But the world, with the mind's assistance, wells up and drowns our core being with the tsunami of karma and illusion.

These floods come to everyone, so we are going to have to build an ark, like Noah and unify all the animal qualities within us to bring them peacefully along. His epithet is "The One God Saved." Humans contain the whole universe. If we can do the spiritual work to bring this inner world to unity and peace, it will be easy to sail the ship of our lives.

Next, we have Abraham. His epithet is "The Friend of God." He's known for his clarity about the One, uncreated God. He's really the father of monotheism. It is believed that Abraham's father was an idol maker. But Abraham had amazing insight that broke through the karma of his time and deliver the message of a single, unseen, formless Deity. So it seems that in Abraham's time, a sufficient number of people had spiritually matured enough to usher in this era of understanding.

Now, Ishmael's epithet is "The Sacrifice of God." Teacher said it was the first born that went through this trial. If you grew up being told it was Isaac, don't get hung up here, we're always looking for the wisdom point, not the history. So the story of Abraham goes that God asked him to sacrifice his son. Why would a benevolent God request such a thing?

Teacher explained that Abraham's attachment to his son rivaled his love for God. It stood between them. We should have some attachment to our offspring, but for the prophets, it can't be greater than the One who created them and ourselves. So the Power of the universe made Abraham aware that he had created, in a sense, an idol of his son. So this trial was actually a mercy from the most Merciful. Of course, Abraham, being surrendered to the will of God, had to go through with it. Teacher said that Ishmael had embraced the order in the knowledge that God had accepted him and was welcoming him back. Of course, being a prophet himself, he was in a state of surrender to God. The story shows that through this intense experience, Abraham reached the required state of detachment, and God ordered the sacrifice of a ram in Ishmael's place. What Abraham had to sacrifice was the attachment of the vacillating mind to the impermanent world. This is also our story: The journey of the dark night of the mind.

We are cutting away what is not God, refining our understanding as life proceeds. What appears to be reality this year, next year we might say, what a fool I was. That's not reality either, and that's the way it goes. And looking back twenty years, we shake our heads. This learning never ends.

Moses is next. "The One Who Spoke To God." He brought the law or the Word. He reached a state where he could receive the commandments. Some of us speak to God, but how good is the connection? The Absolute can hear us, being the original GPS: God pre-installed software! But can we receive accurate and clear guidance back? When someone tells me, "God told me something," I get nervous because Father's example shows us what state of clarity you have to be in for this to happen. Receiving the Word has nothing to do with imagination. It is beyond.

King David, also a prophet, is known as the "Vice-regent of God." Not only was he a king in this world, he was also king of his own heart. He was entirely present, not ruled by the nine openings in his body (two ears, two nostrils, two eyes, a mouth, and the two below the waist, also known as the nine planets that spin our life around.) (I know the world has other things to say about him.) We need the law to control this wayward mind and body. We need the surrender of Ishmael to receive the law. We need the faith of Abraham to reach surrender. Like Noah we need to be saved from the ocean of illusion as it floods our life. And we must choose and be chosen like Adam to go on the path of these stations.

And then, in this stable state, we can receive the station of Jesus, whose epithet is "The Soul of God," not the soul of man. There is only one soul. When Jesus said, "I am the way," we can interpret that to mean through the soul. But this is the selfless path, not egoistic. This doesn't happen through titles, creed, race, nationality, worldly honors, or achievements, and Jesus would never divide the human family into groups of any kind.

And Muhammad is the "Chosen Messenger." Peace and blessings be upon him and all the prophets. Father explained that the messenger meant the light within the soul that is Jesus, saying, "Come this way, come to truth, come within the soul, merge with the Absolute, this is your true inheritance, this life is who you are, everything else will perish." At this destination, there is no longer any you or I. There is only Oneness. The lover and the Beloved once again united in immortality – welcome home.

12

Three propensities
of the mind

The stations of the prophets are part of the human journey, but how will we reach them? To do that we must continue with the Know Thyself Curriculum, which I believe has always run concurrently with the prophets' revelations. This is what I'm calling the journey from the mind to the soul.

Bawa showed us clearly that the mind has three main propensities: monkey mind, the dog of desire, and the baby mind. So what are the antidotes to these three mind culprits? First, becoming aware of them, unmasking the mind as not the essential "me" but what the world grafted onto me. The monkey mind copies anything it sees. "Well, sometimes I see a person with a useful tool that I could use in my work," you might say. OK, that's positive. But what about the "baubles" we see and then want to acquire? Well, there you go. We'll need discernment to decide when the monkey is tricking us. No animal has the level of discernment a human has. That's if we aspire to develop or utilize wisdom-discernment, devoid of desire, fascination, or delusion, etc.

The baby mind goes for the grab. Its tendency is like the baby being pushed past supermarket shelves, reaching out and crying for everything it sees, only satisfied for a few moments with what it's given. But what if patience goes before that? Could a foundation of gratitude also be considered in slowing down the want? If we walk with the consciousness of these qualities and in fact put them out front of us, can we soften the blow of object fascination, allowing discernment to analyze what it is seeing. "Oh, the color is polychromatic gold, wow! What a trick. The old one I have is dull grey, but it still works. Maybe I'll dust it off or spray it." All the manufacturer has done is given it a new look.

I remember wanting an E-type jaguar car when I was young; many boys' dream of my era. (Way out of my reach.) But now they look a bit odd, even clunky. A great design, no doubt, but now it doesn't carry the fascinating stimulus that it did back in the day. Of course, going along with that was the praise and delusional stature that's associated with it.

Today many people wear the marks of a slave. In a crowd of people you'll see the same clothing brand marks on their hats, shoes, jackets, everywhere; it seems we don't really like freedom after all! When discernment filters those out, we make different decisions: more practical, balanced and ultimately more useful and satisfying. Or do we wish to be pushed around by a world of never-ending trinkets and brand pressure? Our choice.

We can be employed the dog of desire for the essentials: food, shelter, and clothing, in *reasonable* proportions. But when it is unrestrained, imagine a dog without a leash. The same troubles experienced or caused by that dog will batter us. For this, Teacher used to talk about the four good qualities of modesty, restraint, prudence and propriety. These four I call the behavioral immune system. They go out ahead of the body, creating a force shield, not to spoil our fun but to protect us.

Many of the religious injunctions appear to be in place to ruin our fun, but it is the dog of desire and the monkey mind that think this. Suppose these injunctions are explained within the system of becoming enlightened or increasing our humanity. In that case, they can function as protection against physical and mental trauma, becoming the leash that slows down the dog of desire.

13

The behavioral immune system (MRPP)

Don't expect modesty, restraint, prudence and propriety to be discussed on television tonight. Will the TV shows reflect these qualities? Are we conscious of how the celebrities' behavior reflects them? Can we remember when we last spoke to our children about modesty, restraint, prudence and propriety, or when our parents mentioned them to us? Can we remember the last time we had a deep conversation with our friends about their significance?

The soul is in the opposite direction to the body because it has no form. The body is not evil but it can stand in the way of enlightenment. Overindulgence in bodily things: sex, vanity, personal appearance, physical beauty, etc., could be seen as evil if they prevent contemplation of the soul. To become a soul being, one must pass one's thoughts, actions and behavior through the filter of modesty, restraint, prudence and propriety. These are the qualities that lead to saintliness.

These are the warrior qualities people need to succeed in holiness. You can't attained righteousness through weapons and the slander of the other. To take on these qualities, you must be a super-warrior, an inner-warrior. Declarations of faith and religion - shouting prophets' names – none of these gets us there. The Divinity does not listen to our tongues or consider which scripture we carry or wave in the air. Do we take It for a fool? Of course we do because most of us have created a foolish god in our own image.

I think the true God, through the soul, in part judges our behavior and thoughts according to how they stack up against modesty, restraint, prudence and propriety. Advertising is not guided by these gracious qualities but by the seven deadly sins: pride, greed, lust, envy, gluttony, wrath, and sloth. In their media studies, are children being taught about this in grade 5? Are their media-protection classes for children in schools? Bawa used to say: "If you don't teach your children to be human, they will be demons!" Will secular humanism be enough to guide the children of the future? What will be its central document? Where will the children go to learn about its tenets? Past and present religion, led by the 1%, has caused many wars and problems.

But on balance I think the majority of people following its tenets have done more good than bad over the millennia, though it's hard to see that sometimes. I'm thinking among the congregants, not the religious authorities that continue to separate the world family.

Once we face the trickiness of this mind with all its machinations, we can see the need to stand guard over it with our wisdom. It's not hard to see how those who have abandoned wisdom or never developed it at all can become the murderers and miscreants of our society. And it's not hard to imagine that Jesus and all the wise ones throughout time would illuminate their close students about how the mind enmeshes us in the ever-changing world of scenes and how liberation lies in understanding and controlling it.

14

Why does God let us suffer?

God doesn't want anyone to suffer at all. Humans were created with the ability to merge with God. The other animals don't have this ability. It is only this state of being, merged with God, where there is no suffering. So, where do you want God to intervene?

There are almost eight billion people. When should He/She intervene in each life: when we drive our cars too fast, go into a bar to drink alcohol, overeat food, start a fight, steal from someone, have evil thoughts about someone? How many times a week should God intervene in each life; five, ten, twenty-five times?

We have free will while in this body. It is our human responsibility to live in peace and help others to live in peace. Millions of people who consider themselves good make guns for a living. Is that righteous action? Humans have become experts at destruction, but we weren't created for that. Don't blame God.

Some say there is no free will and that everything is pre-destined. But God sent prophets and saints to advise and correct us, proving it is not predestined if we can make course corrections. We have to correct our karma and make a real effort to self-improve. (However, not all those born with a human face are human. Bawa.)

We don't have God's big picture view of the three worlds: world of the souls, the Earth world, and the hereafter. From God we come, and to God we return. Sometimes, in the past, when the world was in jeopardy of being destroyed by people, God intervened.

We have been given many rights, but we do not have the right to destroy Nature. God created this world as a place where we can know God. It's not ours to destroy. So much is out of balance now, mainly caused by the wealthy nations whose behavior challenges Nature's many tipping points.

The time of worldwide "biblical scale" correction may be just over the horizon once again. Maybe it has already happened locally in some places! How distant are we from God (Truth)? However far away that determines the degree of suffering.

15

Two or three monotheistic prophet lines

From Abraham's time, thought to be about 1,900 BCE, in what is today the Arabian Peninsula and/or Middle Eastern region of the world, we have two strands of monotheist prophets: those through Isaac (Abraham's Family through Sarah) and those through Ishmael (Abraham's Family through Hagar). More oral tradition from the Isaac side of the family became the Torah, Old Testament. Many, but not all, of those names are familiar to us culminating in the birth of Jesus, son of Mary.

From Ishmael, it seems, there is a less cohesive community, but nevertheless with prophets dotted along the same timeline (Hud, Salih, Shu'ayb), all the way to Aminah and Abdullah giving birth to Muhammad. The tribe into which Muhammad was born is called Quraysh, believed to be descended from Ishmael. And so, there must have been exalted families in the tribe who had kept the belief, tradition, and wisdom necessary to birth a prophet capable of reciting the last great scripture of monotheism.

For me, it's exciting to think that Jesus may have

directly influenced the ancestors of Muhammad during his lifetime. But even if that wasn't so, people in the region were aware of versions of the New Testament for several hundred years after Jesus' death and so were familiar with his mission and teachings. Many Christian settlements were established, even in Ethiopia, by the time of the prophet Muhammad's birth; and of course Jesus and Mary are mentioned prominently in the Koran.

We know that Muhammad's recitation of the Koran, scriptural guidance believed to be the word of God by many, continued throughout his life of 63 years (570 – 633 CE). But concurrent with this, there is something called the Hadith, day to day living and interactive observations collected throughout his life and written down, providing guidance that educates some faithful to this day. I propose that these interactions contain some of the Know Thyself Curriculum of his day.

Over in Persia, modern day Iran, Zoroaster lived around 600 BCE., also considered a prophet in the monotheistic tradition. It is believed he had a tremendous influence on the Judaism of that time, and subsequently, his precepts entered Christianity and Islam. (Encyclopedia of World Religions.) Perhaps this is why the Persians felt some sort of affinity for the Jews in exile in Babylon after they conquered it, and let them return to Jerusalem.

16

God is knowable

Some people think that God is a total mystery and cannot be known. But I'm afraid I have to disagree. True, God contains inconceivable mystery, but we can also know a lot about the nature of God, even through the miniscule amount of words ascribed to Jesus that have come down to us. I say minuscule because my experience with Bawa shows me that realized beings are not slouches. They are selfless beings serving others every day.

At least forty books and documents of Bawa Muhaiyaddeen's discourses have been published, including question and answer sessions and songs. Yes, he often sang about God and wisdom. Thousands of recorded hours not yet published. So, I'm sure if Jesus had been documented fully during his life, an immense body of work would be extant from his tens of thousands of hours of ministry. Many of the conflicting stories in the four New Testaments make no sense to me, but the wise words we have are consistent with the luminaries of other traditions and my own heart, which I think validates them.

Jesus is a servant of God, so the words he speaks are God's. He is always exhorting us to be kind and merciful, "just as thy Father is merciful," to take care of the disadvantaged, to feed the hungry, and help the poor, to "forgive those who trespass against us," to help our neighbor, and more and more leading to a pretty nice world if everyone heeds those words.

So what's happened, people? Are not the law of the jungle, the keeping of human slaves and the oppression of indigenous peoples negated by the parables of Jesus?

In the Koran, God speaks of himself many times with names like the most merciful, most compassionate, the generous one, the all-knowing, the omnipresent, all powerful, the subtle one, the repairer, the patient, the grateful, and the forgiver. The Sufis, throughout time, have recognized ninety-nine names and called them the Asma-ul-husna (Beautiful Names, see back matter for complete list).

Bawa and his students compiled a book of the names with further explanation. These names, to me, are the most extraordinary insight into God's nature we have. They are used for prayer, reciting them many times over while contemplating their meaning and how we can inculcate them into our behavior.

Man is supposed to be in the image of God, I don't think this image is physical, but making these names the basis of our existence helps us become that image.

For the macho males who may think qualities like

compassion and mercy make you appear a weakling, I say this. I acknowledge that goodness without wisdom can get you in trouble. A few women have shared with me over the years how they were good toward their partner, and he abused them. If you do a favor for a wild animal in difficulty, you better not stand around waiting for praise. You better have plotted your retreat because as soon as that animal's pain has subsided, it's thinking of its next meal, and that could be you, depending on the creature.

I don't give money to everyone who stops me on the street begging. They often say they're hungry and need food for a sandwich. I tell them I donated to the Salvation Army just one block away; you can get food there. They'll say I don't like their food. And I'll say that's because you're not hungry, you want money for drugs and you won't get it from me. And I add, the day you become a sincere person and cease lying, your life will improve. And they shrug or curse me and walk off.

I would love to help them, but it is impossible to help people who have gone too far into the dark forest. That's throwing pearls before swine. If you are developing wisdom alongside goodness, you are in control, and it doesn't matter what people are interpreting about you.

17

Seventeen epics

To be conscious of these names, also known as God's qualities, enables us to keep them front and center in our daily lives, staying on the track of God's children for those who care to identify as such. They help us counteract their opposites, which Bawa referred to as the seventeen puranas – not the biting fish, although their effects on our lives are equivalent. Their translation is the seventeen epics, the distilled essences of drama: arrogance, karma, illusion, tarahan, singham, suran (sons of illusion related to the sex act), lust, anger, miserliness, attachment, fanaticism, envy, intoxicants, desire, theft, murder, and falsehood. These seventeen are behind the plots of TV shows, novels and theater, and will also run riot in our life dramas if we don't live the examined life and apply wisdom.

"Good people make bad drama" is a phrase bandied about in writing circles. It's a shame that bad behavior is modeled millions of times in our youth through the media. It has to wear on us or we normalize it, and it even could predispose some toward it. Some of these behaviors are related in ways that create a domino effect. They are the source of much conflict and strife. Any one of them can motivate an entire life, even among what we might call successful people! But like Shakespeare reminds us in Julius Caesar, "The fault, dear Brutus, lies not in our stars but in ourselves, that we are underlings."

And I worry how we will counteract these in a secular society? Will there even be a conscious need to do so? Where will the secular society turn for guidance? Where can the guidance be carved into stone for successive generations to consult? We see those who have lost the positive qualities every day splashed across our news feeds shooting kids in our schools. "If you don't raise the children to be human beings, they will be demons." We are born with divine consciousness at the center of our being, but that's not enough. It has to be nurtured at the same time that the fascinating forces of the "world" are grafted onto us as we grow, making us predominantly "mind beings" when in fact, we were born to be "soul beings."

"When the mind is free, the soul is imprisoned; when the soul is free, the mind is imprisoned." (Bawa.)

18

Illusion

Maya is a Sanskrit word referring to the nature of the creation. Bawa generally used it to mean illusion. Maya is one of those words important enough to become part of our vocabulary. It is how we perceive the world, not the world itself. Even science can now show us that many layers make up the world of form: the macro scale and, deeper still, the atomic structure – atoms (tiny specs of energy) spinning around a nucleus of energy at the speed of light.

I call this electromagnetic fiction, because what we now see as a tree, a body, or a house, is really this atomic structure masquerading as forms. Add to that our perception of these forms seen through our karma (opinions, race, culture, class, prejudices, poverty, misunderstandings, wealth, desires, etc.,) and who could ever call that objective perception, or seeing the world as it really is? Objective perception has become, for me, God's point of view.

Example.

I bought a rundown house in one of the poorer

towns of southeastern Pennsylvania. I've since renovated it; for me, it is a great place. Now someone living in one of the wealthiest neighborhoods, just twenty
miles away, would be depressed if they made some
bad investments, lost their wealth, and were forced
to live in my house, even in its renovated state. This
exact house located in their neighborhood would be
valued many times over, so they would not feel so bad
if it were over there. It is made of the same materials
as other houses, all variations of mud! (Also the same
creatures are constantly eating it!) Wood-mud, stone-
mud, plastic-mud, marble-mud. No material on Earth
didn't come basically from mud!

Can we even imagine that a God would have any
value judgment of this kind? And yet some might even
think that God was punishing them if they fell on hard
times. Has God agreed to take care of our needs, our
wants, or both, or neither? Many people worldwide
have received an immense bounty of material goods,
and some have received little. Once these conditions
happen to us, we get used to them and, in fact, equate
them with life itself. But the materially wealthy person could be living a deluded life and the one without could have divine wisdom. And, of course, the
materially wealthy person could also attain divine
wisdom, while the materially deprived person could
also be deluded. (The poor and the rich boast about
their "exalted states!") God does not play favorites,
but what state of being is preferable to God? Shouldn't

that ultimately be preferable to us?

It is really tough to see through the world we are in, lift its veil, as it were. I remember reading Carlos Castaneda years ago, and he talked about "stopping the world" in one of his books. I thought that was an interesting concept. Now, I realize you cannot stop the world outside yourself, but, to some extent, you can stop it inside yourself. Fasting is one way of doing this. It controls our routine and sets an intention within us, often to the annoyance of the mind, presenting to us what we have gotten into since the last time we questioned our day.

The fast of Ramadan goes for thirty days, eating and drinking only between sunset and sunrise. It is an annual fast and it can act as a course correction. It shows us everything we have been up to for the year. That is, if we are paying the right kind of attention. The point of all this is to suggest that most of us have a hard time seeing things as they really are. I know having a nice house in a decent neighborhood is favorable, but that is not the point. What all these worldly objects and situations do to our state of being is the concern. Ultimately the pursuit and attainment of permanent happiness cannot be contingent on the products from the mud of this world, but if we do connect it to that, that is the point at which we become subject to pleasure and suffering, praise and blame.

This pursuit, I believe, is what has driven Western society to an obsessive life of acquisition. Had our religions, disciplines, philosophies, education, informed us sufficiently, we would have restrained this wild beast to some extent, using wisdom to guide our lives instead of economics. With all the factors of the 21st century coming upon us: the effects of global warming/climate change, water and mineral resource depletion, peak oil production or demand, over-population, totalitarian agriculture, deforestation, etc., tripping the natural world's tipping points, this will force us to assess our lives from a deeper perspective than an economics/acquisition position.

We are just animals in a landscape. When we lose sight of that, and things go wrong, we can be so affected, even to point of ending our lives prematurely. I think you know that I acknowledge our potential exaltedness to be vice-regents of God if we make the effort. But we are subject to whatever other animals confront: floods, droughts, starvation, plagues, etc.

Here's the thing, as animals, all that is required are the three basics that other animals have: food, shelter and clothing. Most animals grow their clothing on their bodies. We probably used to, but now we mainly grow them in the ground (cotton) or extract them from oil and natural gas (polymers) or shave them off other animals (wool from sheep)! And we don't need 5,000 square feet of shelter or 30 garments in the closet, but just enough for modesty and protection.

If you have these three basics, Bawa used to say, you cannot say, "I am poor." Poverty is when you don't have these three, not when you measure yourself against someone living in excess and then consider yourself deprived.

It's a very unreal world we find ourselves in now. We all need to think about this. The whole world runs on dissatisfaction; advertisers tells us constantly that we're inadequate if we don't have their products. Be on guard for these subtle and not so subtle evils. Gratitude is one of God's qualities. The insatiable appetite that advertisers try to install in us is opposite to this. Nowadays, through mass media, we have all been inoculated with the propensities of the 1%. Cultivate moments when you can say to the world, stop; I have enough – that is wisdom and that's radical!

19

Meanwhile, in the courtyard

Meanwhile, about 1,960 years ago, Jesus might be working in a carpentry workshop on the outskirts of Yathrib to help support his living expenses and possibly others, Mary, his mother, having left many years earlier on a mission to a far-off land. Adjacent to the workshop there might be a courtyard big enough to contain a small crowd. At various times during the day and throughout the week Jesus might walk across there and address the crowd according to their questions and needs. The people gathered might consist of nomadic tribes people who were passing that way and heard of his divine knowledge. There would be Jews from the neighborhood. Here and there Nubians who are visiting from across the Red Sea, and Ethiopians too. Certainly, some of the local desert and townspeople descended from the Nabateans and others, including descendants of Ishmael. Maybe there is a trader from India visiting before returning to the nearest port and sailing home.

I would posit that prayers fall into two groups: Praise of God prayers, and shopping prayers – when we ask for things. Most people come to the courtyard for their shopping prayers to be fulfilled like health advice, some hoping for a miracle. Though Jesus stopped doing miracles years earlier because too large a crowd attended, just wanting to be entertained. And then some questioned him on how he did such things, some accusing him of being a magician. This crowd prevented the sincere seekers from accessing him. So now he just gave advice and occasionally laid on hands, and the healing would take place slowly after the people departed.

Sometimes he would tell them to return if it were a big problem. Surprisingly, very few returned to complete the cure. Some would ask wisdom questions. That would please Jesus the most, though he would say it's hard to share wisdom with people if their priority is relieving their backache.

After the general crowd dispersed, the regulars remained, and that's when most of the wisdom teaching occurred. You might say these were his disciples, but he didn't see it like that. He considered himself an elder sharing his life's experience with those less experienced. He never showed any sense of superiority or inequality.

He spoke to them about not taking intoxicants. Some people think that getting high is equivalent to transcendence, but it's not. In that state, you enter a room in the mind that's new and fascinating, but it's a horizontal move, not an ascent to higher consciousness. "And I never turned water into wine," he might say. "Why would I do that? The children wouldn't be able to drink it. I turned brackish water into drinkable water and they said it tasted so good it was like wine. I would never encourage my close companions to consume alcohol and addle their wisdom, especially not in religious ceremonies, which might give it legitimacy."

"No more animal sacrifices for any reason because that time has passed. God can't consume your material sacrifices. Sacrifice your bad qualities, thoughts and actions. We must treat all the animals with care because they have feelings and suffer like us. Haven't you seen how a cow protects her calves and feeds them with patience? Other animals like birds build their own houses (nests) find partners, start families, tend to all their children's needs. Are these dumb creatures?" They have feeling, awareness and intellect, just like humans. But we also have discernment, subtle wisdom, divine analytical wisdom and divine luminous wisdom (Bawa Muhaiyaddeen), not that everyone of us uses those faculties. So many people don't function much above the level of animals.

"Take care of all those in need and help them to take care of themselves." He reminded them of the Ten Commandments often and other aspects of God's law for humans.

During his lifetime he did visit Ethiopia, which was a short boat ride across the Red Sea. He was invited by a local dignitary who had met him on a visit to Yathrib. He ministered to a very receptive audience there and was accompanied on the journey by some Ishmaelite Bedouin.

He talked about how the exodus out of slavery didn't end with Moses but is ongoing. "We are enslaved by almost every desire we have, so much of our lives are beyond reasonableness."

He warned that the further people moved away from the understanding of God, the closer comes the destruction. "You don't have to belong to a religion, but you do need to bring the qualities of God into your thoughts, speech and actions." He spoke about how everything on earth serves something else. "The trees create shade and habitat for others, the rain waters everyone and everything, even the mountain slows the wind to protect people, and that we must find our way to fit into this pattern of God's will, or, being out of step with the divine, we'll suffer the consequences."

Eventually, the body of Yeshua, as Jesus was called during his lifetime, reached its limit. He saw it coming and arranged with his companions to take care of things, and he was buried in the local Jewish cemetery in the customary way.

Then he joined all the other prophets, saints, and enlightened ones, sitting, as it were, shoulder to shoulder at one table in the afterlife. In the way of the prophets, if we don't nurture that sense of unity in our lives, but wish to separate the human family with slander, we are out of step with the will of God.

Meanwhile, in the courtyard

*May God's will be done. Show us the straight path,
the path of those on whom You have bestowed Your
grace. Amen.*

99 Names (Qualities) of God

Many names are similar; I have done my best to compile the clearest list. They may differ slightly from other sources, but you'll get the idea. The names I've marked with an asterisk (*) may baffle a little compared to most of the qualities. Although we should emulate the names of God, we must fully understand these before we emulate them:

Abaser – Humbler; Avenger; Dishonorer; Distresser - Destroyer; Giver of Death; Judge; Restrainer – Binder. Occasionally we may need to restrain someone in our company, but these qualities, when embraced by us, must be applied to our internal struggle, and are not permission to oppress others. We do have to destroy our bad qualities or at least convert them. We'll need to judge ourselves, and the path of transcendence is a constant dying to our old self and becoming renewed. Try reading through the list with deep contemplation in your heart, it's very powerful. For convenience, I've put them in the English alphabetical order, thought they are often in different orders.

Abaser, Humbler (*)
Accepter of Repentance, Ever-relenting
Almighty
All Knowing, Omniscient
All Powerful, Decreer
All Powerful, Determiner
All Seeing
Avenger (*)
Aware One
Beloved, Affection, Loving
Beneficent, Sustainer, Gracious, Compassionate
Benefiter, One Who Grants Favor
Bestower, Giver of Gifts
Bountiful One, Generous
Clement, Forbearing
Comprehensive One
Creator
Delayer, Postponer
Dishonorer (*)
Distresser, Destroyer (*)
Enduring, Everlasting
Enricher
Equitable
Eternal, Absolute
Ever-living, Alive
Exalter
Expander, Widener
Faithful One
Fashioner

Finder
Firm One
First
Forgiver, Absolver
Foremost, Expediter
Friend, Protecting
Gatherer
Giver of Death (*)
Giver of Life
Governor, Ruler
Grateful, Thankful One
Great, Eminent One
Great Forgiver
Guide
Hearer
Hidden, Inner
Highest One
Holy
Honorer
Incomparable, Purpose Setter
Inheritor
Judge (*)
Just
Kind One, Gentle One
King Over All Earthly Kingdoms
King, Sovereign
Last
Light
Lord of Majesty

Maker, Creator
Manifest
Merciful, Compassionate
Mighty One
Most Glorious
Most Great, Self-expanding
Most High
Noble, Glorious
Nourisher, Sustainer
The One
Opener
Originator, Innovator
Overcomer, Subduer, Dominant
Pardoner
Patient One
Peaceful One
Praiseworthy
Preserver
Preventer, Delayer
Protector
Provider
Reckoner
Reconciler
Repairer, All compelling
Responsive One
Resurrecter
Restorer
Restrainer, Binder (*)
Righteous, Pure

Self Sufficient, Rich One
Self-subsisting,
Strong One
Sublime
Subtle
Trustee, Advocate
Truth
Unerring, Right Guide
Unique One
Watchful
Wise
Witness

Further reading, wisdom book recommendations

Bawa Muhaiyaddeen rarely spoke exclusively on one subject but integrated the negative and positive aspects into each talk, creating a tapestry of learning. Most books have a glossary and some are indexed. Titles not by Bawa Muhaiyaddeen will have their authors listed.

Nature of the mind, world and soul - core teachings:

The Guidebook To The True Secret of the Heart, Vol. 1 & 2 and *God, His Prophets and His Children*
When I first heard Bawa Muhaiyaddeen speak, he had already explained many of the Know-Thyself curriculum precepts and he could not re-explain them for every discourse. So these guidebooks are where we all started with the core teachings. The great sorting begins here, and the clarity about the world, soul, mind, God, form versus formlessness, etc., is illuminated. These books contain chapter headings like: Peace, The Mind, The Camera, The Soul, and Beyond Form. Through these talks, I believe you will begin

to see life more accurately. They will inform much of what you do. Your decisions will be informed by extra wisdom, making them more agreeable to your life. I believe all these volumes can enhance any spiritual or philosophic tradition.

Divine Luminous Wisdom That Dispels The Darkness
More of the core teachings with an extensive Q & A section with over a hundred and fifty wisdom exchanges. Especially for those more familiar with the Hindu or Buddhist tradition. These exchanges happened in the early 1970s when Bawa Muhaiyaddeen was centered mainly in the north of Sri Lanka among a predominantly Hindu population. Again the reader would benefit from reading vols. 1 & 2 of the Guidebooks first.

The qualities of God - core teachings:

Asma'ul Husna: The 99 Beautiful Names of Allah
These have been written and explained through the ages. Also called the qualities of God. Qualities like: mercy, compassion, forgiveness, generosity, patience, subtlety, strength, reconciliation, etc. If there is a description of God, this is it. And all the qualities are performable by human beings. These qualities form the essence of the phrase "I (God) created you in my own image." The image is not physical, but the actualization of these qualities.

You can read the list of names as a very potent

meditation exercise. Or, a single name can be recited 3, 11, 33, 99, or 300 times as a form of meditation, as you reflect on and sink in its meaning. There is a great effect on the heart when all 99 are read in one session, with detailed explanations from the book. This volume also contains explanations about the precept of the redirected heart. Several explanations about powerful prayer phrases can help us in our daily lives. This book contains an essential part of the core teachings. Paperback, 4 x 5 3/4", 211 pages. (Fellowship Press)

The Four Relgions - core teachings:

Four Steps To Pure Iman (Faith)

Hinduism/Buddhism, Zoroastrian/Zen, Christianity, Judaism/Islam: One within the four – four within the one. Together these religions form the essence of spiritual completeness and were never meant to be separated. This is His-story, God's story that was revealed for Man's benefit. However, some current interpretations of scripture and traditions may not be divinely inspired, but distortions/additions by self-interested parties. We all have to progress from idol worship to formlessness. Canonical law, the path, divine merging, and gnosis. The four steps to pure faith. They are states of understanding contained within all authentic spiritual traditions. In Hinduism, they are known as, sariyai, kiriyai, yogam and gnanam. In Islam they are known as shariat, tariquat, hakiquat, and marifat. This is the path of progression out of karma and towards the Absolute. This book contains an essential part of the core teachings. Paperback, 5 1/2 x 8", 68 pages. (Fellowship Press) Reading Guidebook Vol. 1 & 2 first would support understanding.

Love - core teachings:

Book of God's Love

A small book with four chapters: True Love, Forgiveness, Cultivating the Heart, Eternal Youth.

In today's world people use the word love to mean so many things. Here we read about a love that is not contingent upon the world. This is the zenith of love from which we can measure all the other attachments. In the chapter on forgiveness, we are left with no doubt as to the nature of God with regard to this subject and therefore our responsibility with it also. This is a very healing chapter. This is a very healing book. I think we can safely say that modern culture is obsessed with eternal youth. This chapter clearly shows that all physical things change and that the only eternity is to be found within. It clearly reveals the correct state to foster eternal youth. It is an observation of mine that those who have the most serene inner state are also those who look the most youthful, even in older age. We keep applying these magic potions to our shell, when youthfulness emanates from within our being. This is a great companion book with The Wisdom of Man. Both books contain essential illumination of the core teachings. Pocket size, 115 pages. (Fellowship Press)

Wisdom - core teachings:

Wisdom of Man (although all the books contain wisdom)

Devotional Songs - core teachings:

Songs of God's Grace

During one of my early visits to Bawa Muhaiyaddeen, he started to sing in the middle of a discourse. This was a bit of a shock to me. No one else seemed surprised, so I soon got over it and listened. Through the vibration of song, many explanations were given. There is a great yearning in these songs. If life has been difficult for you, this is where you will find some soothing balm. Sometimes my mood demands that only the Song Book will fulfill my inner needs. Many of his songs were recorded and are available on CD also. Paperback, 5 1/2 x 8", 154 pages. Reading Guidebook Vol. 1 & 2 first would open up the meaning of the songs further. (Fellowship Press)

Explanatory Discourse - core teachings:

The Fast of Ramadan: The Inner Heart Blossoms

I call this book, The View From the Ocean of

Divine Knowledge. I think the title limits its scope. It was called this because many of the talks were given during the month of Ramadan. Many of these talks actually happened during my first six-month exposure to Bawa's teachings. They were my introduction. Bare in mind that many of his American students had been with him for a few years by this time, so there wasn't the need to explain concepts like 'monkey mind' or 'dog of desire.' For folks like me just coming in the door, I headed for the bookstore and devoured Guidebook Vol. 1 & 2, so that I could catch up with the core teaching references and get more out of these multilayered explanations. That is why I have put it here in the study order. Because if you have read the books that come ahead of this, you will get more out of these talks.

Creation as divine signs - core teachings:

My Love You My Children: 101 Stories for Children of All Ages (Fellowship Press)
 Creation as University
 At one point in our interactions with Bawa Muhaiyaddeen, we mentioned to him the need for wisdom illustrations for our children. What followed were daily outpourings of short stories and mainly analogies using the creation to enlighten us. Although they can be used to communicate ethical and wisdom life principles to children, in this collection we are shown the way of looking at the natural creation as the "verses of the divine." Like the original Aesop's

tales, these texts introduce us to the methodology of seeing each creation as containing a wisdom lesson. Many enlightened teachers throughout time have used the examples of the positive and negative traits of flora and fauna to hone our humanity. This publication shows us how to sift meaning from the creation in order to serve the core teachings. Large paperback, 475 pages. I would say it can be read as a stand-alone book, but the 101 stories and analogies would be more deeply understood after reading Guidebook Vol. 1 & 2. It is a great book to use as a daily or weekly meditation. For example, read an illustration in the evening and then carry the lesson with you for 24 hours or a week. (Fellowship Press)

Come to the Secret Garden: Sufi Tales of Wisdom (Fellowship Press)
> Creation as University
> Another volume of the above.

Prayer:

Dikr: The Remembrance of God (Fellowship Press)

Student/Teacher relationship:

Sheikh and Disciple (Fellowship Press)

Questions and Answer Format:

Questions of Life, Answers of Wisdom, Vol. 1&2 (Fellowship Press)

Divine Luminous Wisdom That Dispels The Darkness (Fellowship Press)

Truth and Light: Brief Explanations (Fellowship Press)

Audio - Visual:

For audio or video go to the Fellowship Press website: http://www.bmfstore.com

More Wisdom Texts:

Tao Te Ching – author: Lao Tzu (Get the Jonathan Star translation)

Conference of the Birds – author: Attar (12th century CE!)
One bird decides to go in search of enlightenment and invites all the other birds to join him. What follows is basically a book of excuses about why they cannot!

The Screwtape Letters – author: C.S Lewis
It is a letter exchange between an older devil and his nephew. It is really a book about how not to be human, masterfully written.

Marcus Aurelius Meditations – author: Marcus Aurelius (2nd century CE)
Deep personal reflections by a man of obvious wisdom who was also leader of an empire.

The Great Divorce – author: C.S. Lewis

A man dies and goes to a kind of purgatory. But once a year the bus goes to heaven on a day trip. If you can lose your resentments and negative qualities, you might gain entry. Many prefer to keep their attachments.

The Bhagavad Gita - an important chapter of the Hindu epic, the Mahabharata. (about 5th century BCE)

It is an incredible explanatory wisdom exchange between Krishna and Arjuna, a warrior.

The Drop That Became The Sea – Yunus Emre (Get the Kabir Helminski & Refik Algan translation) (about 13th century CE)

Sacred poem/songs about the state of humankind and being in the divine presence.

Sufism and Taoism: A comparative study of key philosophical concepts – author: Toshihiko Izutsu

So well written, sets the standard for spiritual language.

The Essential Rumi – translation: Coleman Barks

A large volume covering many subject categories from the 13th century mystic Rumi, one of the most read poets in America today.

One Song – author: Michael Green

For those who are visually oriented, view mystical artist Michael Green's numinous illustrations and sayings in this volume. And/or, The Illuminated Rumi.

The Book of Mirdad – author: Mikhail Naimy

An interesting story with teaching, dramatizing the demise of a spiritual community.

The Cloud of Unknowing – Author unknown (about 13th century, maybe Julian of Norwich)

Gnosis level instructions, from a spiritual teacher, conveyed to a novice.

Dark Night of the Soul – author: John of the Cross (16th century) (Get the Mirabai Starr translation)

I recommend a subscription to Parabola magazine: www.parabola.org

Glossary

Brain: The physical organ used by the soul and the mind to communicate with the world and fulfill their intentions. (As distinguished from the mind.)

Divine Light: Not a manifested light but an emanation of divine power; illumination.

Ego: The mind's collective will.

Five Elements: Earth, fire, water, air, ether (not the table of elements which are contained within these). For our purposes these are the building blocks of everything in the universe.

Gnosis: The highest form of divine wisdom. The state of living from within wisdom.

God: The uncreated, omnipresent, omniscient, omnipotent, power of the universe.

Karma: The ethical, moral and physical consequences of thought and action. Used here mainly as negative influences.

Man: Man vs. people or men and women. The natural, genderless divine state of men and women.

Maya: It is used here to mean illusion.

Mind: The mind is an ideational projection of the elements that make up the body, to and from the elements that make up the world.

Prophet: A person who brings a part of God's ongoing story or revelation. They are never separate from God.

Religion: The institutional organizations or cultural expressions that claim to represent a scripture revealed by one or more prophets.

Saints: Those who have transformed themselves using the revelations of the prophets and the "Know Thyself Curriculum."

Sakti: The sakti (energy plus perception, not necessarily accurate perception) that emanates from the created things. This informs the mind.

Soul/Inner-heart: The soul is uncreated and cannot be corrupted. It is a ray of God's 'light,' Life itself, a distinguished intelligence center, sensed in the heart area, drawing its wisdom from the divine. The soul, as compared to the mind, is universal, whereas each mind can have its own propensities.

The Path: The journey from the surface of the eye (the world) into the soul, where we become one in God consciousness.

Wisdom: The evolving ability to access objective reality, or God's point of view. Wise judgment.

Index